T0116433

Outside
is Where
I'd Rather Be

and Other Poems for Kids Like Me

Lorraine L. Hollowell

Order this book online at www.trafford.com
or email orders@trafford.com

Most Trafford titles are also available at major online book retailers.

Printed in the United States of America.

ISBN: 978-1-4669-9012-8 (sc)
ISBN: 978-1-4669-9011-1 (e)

Trafford rev. 04/12/2013

 www.trafford.com
North America & international
toll-free: 1 888 232 4444 (USA & Canada)
phone: 250 383 6864 ♦ fax: 812 355 4082

This book is dedicated to my family
and friends, both near and far.

Table of Contents

Where's My Neighbor's Sister?

I can't find my neighbor's sister.
Could that girl have run away?
She's hiding somewhere, and I miss her.
Oh, why won't she come out to play?

I want to chase her with my spider.
I want to put glue in her hair.
I want to trick her into sitting
On my rubber snake in her rocking chair.

The other day she played with me.
Together we had tons of fun.
I chased her for at least an hour.
Boy! That girl can really run!

Oh where, oh where is my neighbor's sister?
I wish she'd come out and play with me.
We'd have lots of fun together.
I wonder . . .
Where could that girl be?

Brave Little Dave

Everyone thought Little Dave was brave
When he ventured alone inside that cave.
He knew not what lurked inside of it,
But he showed no fear . . . not one little bit.

He loved a challenge and boldly walked in.
He even walked in with a big, fat grin.
His chest was poked out, and his head was held high.
He strutted with confidence . . . was such a brave guy!

A few made a bet that Dave wouldn't do it,
But Little Dave said there was just nothing to it.
He would win that bet, and all his friends knew it.
He'd stay in that cave; yes, he would do it!

And for ten long minutes, he stayed in that cave.
That was all it would take to show Dave was brave.
And he won that bet 'cause he stayed in that cave—
The cave that some say was really a grave.

But Dave didn't come out the way he went in.
He came out flying as fast as the wind!
And when he came out, he lacked that fat grin,
And he said that he'd never go in there again!

Lorraine L. Hollowell

Lost Mom

Yesterday at half past four,
I lost my mom in the grocery store.
I knew that she'd be terrified
Not having me close by her side.

Alone, lost, and away from me,
She was probably as frightened as she could be.
I had to find her someway, somehow,
So I walked up and down every single aisle.

I saw lots of moms and a few dads too.
I saw Mrs. White and Mr. Blue.
I saw two crying babies and my neighbor, Tom,
But nowhere in the store did I see my mom.

But I knew she was somewhere inside that store,
And I knew I'd find her; I was pretty sure.
Mom had to be in there . . . somewhere nearby.
Then suddenly I heard a cry.

It came from Mom running down an aisle.
She looked horrified; she looked plain wild!
She was shaking like a leaf . . . . was so uptight!
She was yelling my name, and her face was white.

When Mom saw me, she quickly ran my way.
How glad I was to find my lost mom that day!
She picked me up and held me tight.
She squeezed my body with all her might!

She cried, "Please don't ever leave me!
Don't wander away! You're only three!"
I promised to never again let her out of my sight,
And she finally calmed down; she ended up alright.

Lorraine L. Hollowell

When Mom's Away

When Mom's not here I rock in her chair
Like it's some kind of horse.
I'd never rock in her chair that way
If she were home, of course.

When she's away I jump and play
Upon her queen-sized bed.
I jump so high, so very high
The ceiling nearly bumps my head!

I eat the things I shouldn't eat—
Goodies, both salty and sweet.
Whatever my mom considers junk . . .
These things are the things I eat.

When Mom's not here,
I slip and slide
All over the kitchen floor.
Sometimes I slip;
Sometimes I slide
Right out the kitchen door.

I love to have
My mom at home.
It's fun when she is near,
But there's one thing
I must admit:
It's more fun
When she's not here!

My Memory

I seldom remember
To pick up my toys,
But I *never* forget
To skateboard with the boys.

I always remember
To play in the park,
But I *often* forget
To come home before dark.

I recall how to climb trees
And to play basketball,
But I can't remember
My math facts at all!

I remember all jokes
That I think are pure funny,
But I completely forget
When I owe my friends money.

At least I remember important things,
So my memory's not all *that* bad.
It's just that the things that I often forget
Seem to make some people mad.

Lorraine L. Hollowell

Who Am I?

I've got a case of amnesia.
Can't remember who I am!
Is my name Nick or Matthew?
Could it be Michael or Sam?

Am I a teacher or a mailman?
A hotel manager who collects rent?
There's even a chance that I might be
The US President!!

Am I Glen, the cook or Sneaky, the crook?
Could I be a tailor named Bob?
Oh mercy me! A thought came to me . . .
I might not have a job!

I was knocked out cold a week ago.
It erased all memory from me.
I'd like to know just who I am.
Who on earth could I possibly be?

I'm Not Sure, My Friend

I'm not sure when we met, my friend,
But it was on the fourth of May.
I don't know where we met, my friend,
But we met at the Chesapeake Bay.

I can't remember what you were wearing then,
But you had on a long, purple dress.
I don't recall your name at all.
But, I'm certain your name is Bess.

Lorraine L. Hollowell

Still a Baby

My sister still wears diapers,
Still wears a tiny bib,
Still drinks from a bottle,
And still sleeps in a crib.

She still sits in a highchair,
Still crawls but doesn't walk,
Still makes funny noises . . .
I just wouldn't call it talk.

I'll be glad when she is old enough
To run and play with me,
But right now my twin sister
Is still just a baby.

Leave Your Sister Alone!

Mom said . . .
"Leave your sister alone!
Come out of her room!
Stop chasing her around
With that worn-out broom!"

And I said . . .
"But she started it, Mom!
Believe me! She lied!
She stepped on my foot
And hit me in the side!"

Then Mom said,
"But your sister would *never*
Do a mean thing like that!
She's an angel from heaven,
And that is a fact!"

Lorraine L. Hollowell

Then I said,
"But that angel from heaven
Came up to me.
She pinched my right leg
Then kicked my left knee!
She said that I pinched *her*,
But she's telling a fib.
Why, she's been a monster
Since leaving her crib!"

Then Mom said,
"But she's only two,
And you're nearly ten.
Now, leave her alone!
I won't say it again!"

So I ask . . .
Nearly ten-year-old readers,
What would you do
If your two-year-old sisters
Did these things to you?

Bully Jim

There once was a kid in my class.
We called him Bully Jim.
Every single one of us
Was extremely afraid of him.

When boys passed Jim, he'd stomp their toes,
And girls . . . he'd pull their hair.
He did such evil things to us,
But our teacher was unaware.

Although we were afraid of him,
We wouldn't tell a soul
Until the day that Bully Jim
Pushed me down a hole!

That kid jumped in right after me
And punched me in the nose.
Did he stop there? Not Bully Jim!
He then stepped on my toes!

Lorraine L. Hollowell

He had the nerve to threaten me.
He told me not to tell.
He said that if I'd tell on him,
He'd push me down a well.

But I went straight to Mrs. Wood
And showed her my dirty clothes.
I showed her bruised-up body too:
My swollen toes and nose.

"Mrs. Wood!" I cried, "Jim bullied me
And dare me to tell on him!"
She replied, "Don't worry, dear.
We'll soon take care of Jim."

When they took Jim away that day,
We kids all breathed a sigh.
We want the very best for him,
But we're glad he went bye-bye.

Now kids, take this advice from me:
If there's a bully in your class,
Just run and tell your teacher.
Just run and tell her fast!

Wiggling Willie Wiggle

I sure would like to know
Why Willie Wiggle
Is wiggling so.
He's sitting in class
In front of me,
And his wiggling's
Driving me crazy!

He's wiggling up.
He's wiggling down.
Willie's wiggling all around.

He's wiggling in.
He's wiggling out.
Willie's wiggling all about.

He's wiggling here.
He's wiggling there.
That kid is wiggling
Everywhere!

I can't concentrate one bit
Due to Willie's wiggling fit.

Lorraine L. Hollowell

Booboo and Bubba

In this corner of the room
Near my teacher's desk
Sits a boy named Booboo—
Booboo, the class pest.

And in this corner of the room
Whistling a strange sound
Sits a boy named Bubba—
Bubba, the class clown.

Booboo and Bubba aren't that bad
Whenever they're apart,
But when they come together
The class nightmare starts!

I Lost My Temper

I had planned to stay on *green* that day-
To obey each rule in every way.
Nothing would cause me to go astray,
But then I lost my temper.

I came in and put my things away.
I copied the homework assigned that day.
I even shared my crayons with Ray,
But then I lost my temper.

I was diligently doing my morning work
Without complaining or being a jerk.
Then Ray decided to make fun of my shirt.
That's when I lost my temper!

Shortly, I was moved
From *green* to *red*
And was sent to the office . . .
To Mr. McLed.
Yes, I'd planned to be good,
But I ended up bad . . .
When I lost my temper.

I should have ignored
Ray that day.
I should have turned
The other way.
Now, for two days, at home,
I must stay
Because I lost my temper.

Lorraine L. Hollowell

Looking for My Temper

I lost my temper three days ago.
Where it went, I just don't know.

Somehow it got away from me
When I played checkers with my friend, Bea.

I thought that *I* was going to win
Before Bea jumped two of my men.

When she got two kings instantly,
It released the temper inside of me.

My temper decided it would get lost,
But I'll show my temper that *I'm* the boss!

I plan to find it and bring it home,
And I'm determined not to let it roam . . .
Again.

Chuckles Cracks His Knuckles

Chuckles likes to crack his knuckles.
It's such an irritating sound!
The more I ask him not to do it,
The more he cracks them, I have found.
I'm sure he does it to annoy me
'Cause he cracks them less when I'm not around.
Oh, how I wish he'd stop that cracking!
I just can't stand that cracking sound!

Lorraine L. Hollowell

Betty Never Blinks

I have a friend named Betty Blyes
Who never, ever blinks her eyes.
She closes them when she sleeps at night,
Then opens them in the morning light.
But from morning to night I've recognized
That Betty never blinks her eyes.

Falling

Last night I dreamt I was

F
  A
    L
      L
        I
          N
            G

Was I on the edge of my bed?
I tried and tried to wake myself up.
So afraid I'd land on my head!

But I just kept on . . .

        Lorraine L. Hollowell

In the dark like a tumbling kite.
I believe I'd still be

F
  A
    L
     L
      I
       N
        G

If Dad hadn't turned on the light.

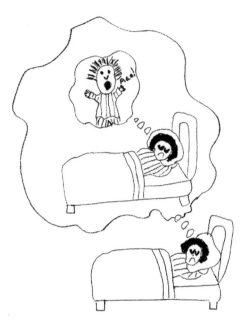

Double Dreaming

I had a dream inside a dream.
I dreamt that I was dreaming.
In the dream inside my dream
I dreamt that I was screaming.

Sleep

I couldn't wait to crawl in bed,
To relax my body and rest my head,
To go to bed and turn out the light,
To close my eyes and sleep through the night,
But I couldn't sleep 'cause I was too uptight.

Lorraine L. Hollowell

Sleeping

Some folks sleep on their tummies
Whenever they go to bed.
Some on their sides . . . some on their backs . . .
But me?
I sleep on my head.

Marshmallow Pillows

I ate two huge marshmallows
Last night in my dream.
They were filled with banana pudding
And covered with blueberry cream.

When I woke up this morning,
I let out a real big yawn.
Then I looked beneath my head
And discovered my two pillows gone.

Lorraine L. Hollowell

What Test?

What test, Miss West?
I must confess:
I didn't study
For a *science* test!

Oh, pleeasse, Miss West!
Not a science test!
I'll be in a mess
If I take *this* test!

May I skip this test?
This science test?
Next time I'll study.
I'll do my best.

What?
A *history* test?
Not another test!
Oh, no, Miss West!
Not a *history* test!!

Outside is Where I'd Rather Be

Math and reading are not for me.
They're almost as bad as history.
Remembering dates can be such a bore.
Does it matter what happened in '64?

I don't spell well, and I hate to write.
Those subjects get me so uptight!
Is it *e* before *i* or *i* before *e*?
Does it really matter which follows *c*?

If you'll let me go outside to play,
I'll do my best out there today.
I'll catch, and kick, and hit the ball—
Climb monkey bars and never fall!

I'll outrun every kid in class.
These legs of mine are mighty fast!
Outside is where I'd rather be.
The classroom's not the place for me!

Lorraine L. Hollowell

Put Your Coat On!

Freddie, put your coat on now!
You could catch the flu!
Don't you realize it's cold out here?
Child, what's wrong with you!?

Do you think you're a snowman?
Are you a block of ice?
Put your coat on and button up!
Please take my advice!

Take Your Coat Off!

Take that coat off, Freddie!
Do you want to roast?
Don't you realize it's warm in here?
Are you are slice of toast?

Just looking at you makes me hot,
So take that coat off now!
How can you wear that thing in here?
Tell me, Freddie. How?!

Lorraine L. Hollowell

The Perfect Room

I changed classes three times today—
From Mrs. Hall, Mr. Bea, to Mrs. Gray.

Mrs. Hall's room was an oven!
Mrs. Gray's was the North Pole!
Mrs. Hall's room was much too hot!
Mrs. Gray's was much too cold!

But I was in a room today—
The perfect room for me.
That's where I got to go and have
P.E. with Mr. Bea.

It was freezing when I got there,
But it warmed up a lot!
And I really didn't mine at all
When it got super hot!

EJ's Desk

EJ's desk is such a mess!
It's the messiest in our room!
Whenever he's told to clean it out,
He has to get a broom.

There're at least ten rocks inside his desk,
And marbles, a whole lot more!
Inside his desk are sunflower seeds
That keep falling on the floor.

In his desk are broken crayons
And an empty crayon box,
A rubber snake, a bouncy ball,
And a little plastic fox,

Lorraine L. Hollowell

Crumpled papers, five library books,
A chocolate bar or two,
A baseball cap, three pairs of socks,
And one smelly tennis shoe!

In EJ's desk is a rotten orange.
It's been there since last week.
There's a little box of apple juice.
Guess what? It's sprung a leak!

Inside his desk is a tiny toy car
And a tiny airplane too,
And with all those jungle toys in there,
His desk is like a zoo!

Yes, EJ's desk is such a mess!
As messy as can be!
But he doesn't have the messiest desk
'Cause that desk belongs to me.

There's a Worm in My Oatmeal

There's a worm in my oatmeal!
It's wiggling all about.
I don't know how it got there.
I've tried to spoon it out.

My mom thinks that I'm joking,
But I'm really not.
She insists I eat this oatmeal
While it's still nice and hot.

It's true . . . I don't like oatmeal,
But neither do I like worms,
And I bet the wiggle worm in this bowl
Is carrying a zillion germs!

Lorraine L. Hollowell

Must I Eat this Oatmeal?

Must I eat this oatmeal?
May I have French toast instead?
Or a plump and juicy sausage
On a slice of buttered bread?

Oatmeal might be good for you,
And it might be good for Dad.
But is it really good for me?
Is ice cream all that bad?

We had oatmeal yesterday
And oatmeal the day before.
I just can't eat another drop.
Please don't give me anymore!

No Olives Please

I'll eat pepper
That makes me sneeze—
Even onions
That make me cry.

I'll eat cornbread
That makes me cough,
But give me olives,
And I might die!

Hot Biscuits

Out of the oven . . .
Onto my plate . . .
Smells so good!
So hard to wait!

Spread the butter
And then the jelly.
Inside my mouth
And down my belly!

Lorraine L. Hollowell

When Judy Eats Beef Stew

Whenever Judy eats beef stew,
She always eats a bone or two.

She sure must have some real sharp teeth
'Cause she eat bones like most eat meat.

At the Restaurant

Mom had lobster,
Dad had steak,
But I had a hotdog
On my plate.

Mom carefully ate
Her lobster.
Dad slowly ate
His steak.
But I gobbled down
The hotdog
That sat upon my plate.

Pooped Brain

My teacher has given me homework galore,
But my brain feels it just can't work anymore.
When I come home, my brain wants to rest.
It's focused all day, and it's done its best.
At home, adding's a nightmare and subtracting's a shame.
And solving word problems is a terrible pain!
My brain wants to leave all that hard work behind,
And homework's the last thing it has on its mind.

Dynamite Excuse

My brother turned
Into dynamite
And blew my homework up
Last night.
He blew up my math
And science too.
But I'll do it tonight;
I promise you.
Trust me, Miss Furman.
Would I lie to you?

Lorraine L. Hollowell

The Flipperdee

There's a flipperdee up in a tree
On a branch in my backyard.
Those poke-a-dot flippers atop his head
Sure make him look quite odd.

He flips around from branch to branch.
He flips from stem to stem.
I've tried to show him to my friends,
But they claim they can't see him.

Today he flipped out of the tree
And landed on the ground.
I tried to catch him with my net
As he flipped all around.

He finally flipped back in the tree.
His flipping just wouldn't stop.
He flipped and flipped and flipped some more
Until he reached the top.

How I wish that I could catch him!
If I could catch him with my net,
I'd be the only kid in town
With a flipperdee for a pet.

Are there Others?

Could there be . . .
I wonder . . .
Life in outer space
On a planet far away-
Another kind of race?

Are there other creatures
Not at all like us
Far beyond our galaxy
Made of glass and rust?

Rather than walk here and there
On two legs like we do,
Could these rusty, glassy creatures
Use one leg instead of two?

Lorraine L. Hollowell

Maybe they don't walk at all.
Perhaps they float around.
Just imagine them floating sideways
As they travel up and down.

Could there be others . . . I wonder . . .
With two noses and one eye?
Other beings with feathered wings
And propellers that help them fly?

Perhaps beyond our universe
There are creatures twelve feet tall.
Or maybe there are others
That are very, very small.

Could others be an inch or two?
Or maybe even smaller?
Twelve feet is mighty tall to me!
Could there be others much, much taller?

Is there another planet
Where the habitats eat weird things
Like cherry-mops and hairy-tops
And fling-a-ting-a-lings?

Are we the only beings,
Or are others out there too
That eat, and talk, and breathe and walk
Just like me and you?

I wonder . . .

The Land of Leaves

Have you been to the *Land of Leaves*—
Where leaves fall, but there are no trees?
Leaves of all shapes and colors too—
Square leaves, round leaves, pink and blue.

Come with me and bring a rake.
Huge pile of leaves, we will make.
We'll jump on them and have such fun!
We'll throw them high as we rip and run.

Lorraine L. Hollowell

Time

Time . . .
Where does it go?
I'd like to know.

Does it float in the air?
Is it out there somewhere?
Does it really fly
Like a bird in the sky?

From seconds to minutes,
From minutes to hours,
From hours to days,
Time never stays.

But . . .
Where does it go?
Would you, too, like to know?

I took a Cuckoo Clock Apart

I took a cuckoo clock apart
And tried to put it back,
But when I reassembled it,
There was something that it lacked.

Now, it won't make that ticky sound,
Or the tocky sound, as well,
And instead of going, "Coo-coo, coo-coo,"
It says, "U-fail, u-fail."

Lorraine L. Hollowell

I'm going to be a Teddy Bear

My sister wants to be a doctor,
My brother, an engineer.
But me?
I can't wait until
I'm a full-grown teddy bear!

My father and mother are teachers.
I wouldn't want that career!
The only thing I want to be
Is a full-grown teddy bear!

I'm going to be a Spaceship

When
I
Grow
Up
I'm going to be a spaceship . . .
Not a kite, an airplane, or balloon,
And when I'm grown, and I've become
A spaceship . . .
I'll get
To visit
That
Man
Living
On
The
Moon!

Lorraine L. Hollowell

Buckle Up

Whether the car's going near,
Or whether the car's going far,
Be sure to buckle your seatbelt
When you get into the car.

Don't waste a bit of time.
Just buckle up real quick,
And when the ends of the belt meet,
Make sure you hear a *click*.

Don't ride away without that *click*.
Take it wherever you go—
Whether the car's moving fast,
Or whether the car's moving slow.

I'll Buckle Up

I didn't put on my seatbelt
Before Dad left the yard.
No, I didn't buckle up that day,
And that wasn't very smart.

Dad slammed into our mailbox.
It was just outside our yard.
And when he slammed into that thing,
He slammed into it hard!

I flew out the window-
The rear window of our car!
I got a cut on my forehead
And one on my dimpled jar.

From now on I'm going to buckle up
When I hop into a car
'Cause an accident can happen
Without traveling very far.

Lorraine L. Hollowell

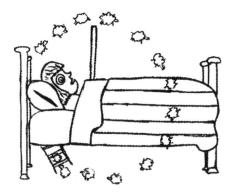

Counting Sheep

I've tried my best to fall asleep
By counting over a thousand sheep.
All kinds of sheep have jumped the fence,
But instead of relaxing, it's made me tense!

I've seen fat sheep jump and skinny ones too.
I've seen white sheep jump; I've seen black and blue.
I've seen sad sheep, glad sheep,
Good sheep and bad sheep.
I've seen every kind of fad sheep—old and new.

Yet, I'm still as awake as I can be.
What has counting sheep really done for me?

Jumping on the Bed

Ahhh shucks!
It's time for bed!
I'd rather jump on the bed instead.

Do I really have to go to sleep?
May I please do just one more leap?

Jumping and leaping is so much fun!
Come and join me, everyone.

Mom and Dad and Baby, too!
Let's jump and leap the whole night through!

Lorraine L. Hollowell

My Shoe Laces

I tie my laces before school starts.
By the time I get to school, they've come apart.

Mom ties my laces real tight for me.
She can tie them before I count to three.

But when I try to tie them fast and tight,
Somehow I just can't get it right.

My peers say I should be ashamed of me
Since I'm the principal and nearly fifty-three.

Carolyn Jace's Untied Laces

Carolyn Jace entered a race
Wearing an untied shoe.
She tripped over her lace
And fell on her face
And began to feel quite blue.

Carolyn Jace entered another race
Again with a shoelace untied.
Shortly she tripped
And fell on her hip,
And she cried, and she cried, and she cried.

When Carolyn Jace now enters a race,
Her shoes are tied tightly for sure!
With two tied shoelaces
She wins *all* the races
'Cause she doesn't fall anymore.

Lorraine L. Hollowell

Keith's Body

Keith's body plays music all day long.
It's either snapping its fingers
Or singing a song.
It's either whistling a tune
Or tapping its feet.
Keith's body is forever beating a beat!

Marc Tu-Chee

I once knew a kid named Marc Tu-Chee.
He was the funniest kid that I knew-chee.
His jokes were so funny
That he told them for money.
Now Marc is both funny and rich too-chee.

Dad's on the Phone

"Rinnnnng!"
Went the phone.
"Hello,"
Said Dad,
And then Dad said,
"Well, that's too bad."

"Okay,"
He said,
"That's fine with me,"
And then Dad said,
"Yes, I agree."

"Of course!"
Dad said,
Then, "Yes . . . yes . . . no."
And then he said,
"I've got to go."

But, before hanging up,
Dad said,
"Good-bye."
Again the phone rang,
And Dad said,
"Hi."

Lorraine L. Hollowell

Grandma's Dustless House

My grandma's house is dustless.
Not a speck of dust in sight!
She dusts every morning.
She vacuums every night.

She sweeps and mops the kitchen floor,
Then waxes shiny clean.
She has the cleanest kitchen floor
That I have ever seen!

She really hates the sight of dust.
It makes her cough and sneeze.
It gives her a congested nose.
It makes my grandma wheeze.

There's no dust in Grandma's closets,
No dust found on her bed,
No dust on chairs or table—
"No dust!" my grandma says.

You won't find dust in her living room,
Her bathrooms or her den.
If dust comes knocking at her door,
She just won't let it in!

My Brother Hates Taking Pictures

Photographers all try their best
To make my brother smile,
But they can't make him smile at all,
Not even for a little while.

He shouts, "No!" when he sees a camera.
He pouts and stomps his feet.
He sure hates taking pictures!
But me? I think it's neat.

Mom combs his hair so perfectly.
He wears his Sunday best,
But it doesn't do a bit of good.
He still acts like a pest!

Lorraine L. Hollowell

The photographers make funny faces.
Some act just like a clown.
Some even try to tickle him,
But all he does is frown.

Me? I love taking pictures!
It's fun just saying, "Cheese."
It doesn't bother me at all.
Taking pictures is *such* a breeze!

In every picture I've taken
I'm wearing my biggest smile.
My brother's pictures, on the other hand,
Are pictures of a child gone wild.

If I was what I Ate

If you are what you eat as some people say
Then I was two slices of bacon today.

I was buttery, syrupy covered pancakes,
And strawberries and milk in a bowl of cornflakes.

I was a cheeseburger covered with relish and mustard,
Some French fries, a peach, and a cup of lime custard.

I was an oven baked chicken leg and
Some creamy potatoes,
Sweet, yellow corn and two cherry tomatoes,

A chocolate chip cookie and vanilla ice cream.
Oh, I was such yummy . . . such good-tasting things!

I was so tasty . . . as tasty could be!
I'm amazed that someone didn't try to eat me.

Lorraine L. Hollowell

Corny

Would you like to know
How he did it?
Then I will tell you how.

I'll tell you just how Corny
Became a popcorn child.

He ate tons and tons
Of popcorn—
Much more than an awful lot!

And after eating all
That popcorn,
His body began to pop.

Rotten Apple

This is such a rotten apple!
Rotten to the very core!

It has brown spots on the outside.
Inside, I'm sure they're more.

A worm is crawling out of it.
Another is crawling in.

Or maybe it's the same wiggly worm
Crawling in and out again.

Lorraine L. Hollowell

Shrimp Rash

Oh, why did I eat that shrimp last night?
Since dinner my skin has not been right.
There's a pinkish rash all over me,
And it sure itches terribly!

I've scratched and scratched and made it worse.
It doesn't matter that Mom's a nurse.
I'm covered with pink lotion from head to toe,
But this itch! This itch still itches so!

I'll never again eat another shrimp!
I'd trade this rash for a terrible limp!
Why, I'd rather fall into nasty green slime
Or even do homework in the summertime!

I don't' like this rash, as you can see,
Or the shrimp that gave this rash to me.

But . . . You're Sick!

When you sneeze, please turn the other way.
Oh, please don't give me your germs today!
Your nose is running; your eyes are red.
Why are you even out of bed?

You look terrible; must have the flu!
Do you want me to get it too?
Doctor, why are you examining me
When you're as sick as you can be!?

Aaa Choo!

Aaa choo! Aaa choo!
My nose just blew,
But it didn't blow away.
No matter how much
My nose aaa choos,
My nose is here to stay.

Lorraine L. Hollowell

Slow Mo

Daddy calls my brother *Fast*.
Mommy calls him *Flash*.
My sister calls him *Quick*.
And me? I call him *Dash*.

But his name is really none of these.
His name is actually *Mo*,
And he isn't really fast at all.
In fact, he's rather slow.

It takes Mo about an hour
To brush and comb his hair.
Last night it took him two hours
To get off of Daddy's chair.

He misses the bus if it's on time,
But also when it's late.
Mo never likes to hurry up.
But he sure does like to wait!

We nicknamed Mo these *speedy* names.
Hoping faster, he would move.
But it appears that neither one
Has helped *Slow Mo* improve.

Slader, the Procrastinator

Slader is a procrastinator.
He won't do it now,
But he'll do it later.

Since I've known him,
He's been a waiter.
Yes, Slader is a procrastinator!

He'll take a raincheck.
He'll drag his feet.
He thinks postponing
Is kind of neat.

He dawdles;
He puts off;
He delays.
What takes some minutes
Takes Slader days.

Lorraine L. Hollowell

Spit It Out!

Spit that gum out immediately!
And don't put it in your desk!

I glanced in there this morning.
Oh, what a gummy mess!

And don't pretend to spit it out.
In your mouth, it mustn't stay!

Remember, I am
Watching you,
So throw that gum away!

Don't blow another bubble!
Don't pop another pop!

Drop it in that
Trashcan now!
Your chewing's got to stop!

As Good As New

I've had this gum for two weeks now,
But it's as good as new.
Its sweetness may be gone away,
But it's still good to chew.

Grandpa's Teeth

Grandpa's teeth are somewhere—
Somewhere inside his house,
But he can't find them anywhere
According to his spouse.

His spouse, of course, is Grandma.
She says his teeth are gone.
Too bad 'cause he can't eat a thing
Without his dentures on.

They both have looked all over-
All over for those teeth,
And Grandpa's getting so upset
'Cause tonight they're having beef!

They weren't under Grandpa's pillow
Nor underneath his bed.
If Grandma's eyes weren't so bad,
She'd find them on his head.

Lorraine L. Hollowell

Fadale, the Barber

Fadale Harber is a barber.
He cuts all kinds of hair.
Be it long, or short, or wavy,
He will sit you in his chair . . .

And he'll cut it like you like it.
Just tell him what you'd like.
Do you want the corners cut low?
Upon your head, shape out a bike?

Would you prefer the "Beatle" style?
It looks something like a bowl.
Is a Mohawk what you'd rather have?
He cuts them perfectly, I've been told.

Fadale Harber shapes up afros
Like no other barber can.
Just try him if you're looking for
The greatest barber in the land!

My Uncle has a Hairy Chin

My uncle has a hairy chin,
But atop his head is bald.
He doesn't have a strand of hair
Atop his head at all.

His beard is nearly two feet long.
It grows and grows and grows!
But absolutely nothing grows
Half a foot above his nose.

I hope that when I'm all grown up,
I won't be as bald as he.
But some say I can bet on it
Due to heredity.

Lorraine L. Hollowell

Three Treats in One

Two mice were scampering near a lake
When they came upon a rattlesnake.

One asked the snake, "How do you do?"
"I'm fine," he replied, "since I met you."

He rattled once; he rattled twice,
And in one gulp, he ate both mice.

An eagle flying high in the air
Saw what happened to the mice down there.

She exclaimed, "This is my lucky day!
Three treats in one! Hip, hip, hooray!"

Which Homophone?

Eye always right the wrong homophone.
Eye really don't no why.
Is it *road* or *rode, hear* or *here,*
Is it *by* or *bye?*

Eye don't no when two right *end* or in
Or when two right *bare* or *bear.*
Eye don't no when too right *through* or *threw*
Or when to right *hare* or *hair.*

I just can't remember witch which two right.
These words confuse me sew!
Whenever eye think eye've got it write,
My teacher says, "Know, know, know!"

The Sock Fairy

Socks just don't disappear.
They reside in *Sock Land* far away from here.

The *Sock Fairy* comes and takes them away.
She took two of my socks just yesterday.

She removes socks from dryers in the dark of the night,
But sometimes she removes them in broad daylight.

As soon as the socks are all fluffy and clean,
Through a hidden tunnel, she takes them,
In the drying machine.

She only takes socks 'cause they come in a pair,
So I guess some other fairy's taking my underwear.

Staying Up

In nineteen hundred eighty-three,
I climbed at the top of an old oak tree.

For several years, I've heard Mom call,
But I'm afraid to move at all.

Provide an elevator, and I'll take the trip,
But climbing down? I just might slip!

So I'm staying here at the top of this tree
Unless someone comes up and recues me.

Lorraine L. Hollowell

Popped by a Pea

Mom bought some brand new hangers.
She put them on my bed.
"Hang up your clothes; clean up this room!"
My dear old mother said.

"Do I have to, Mom?" I pleaded.
"I like my room this way."
"Clean up this room!" she said again.
"Immediately! Don't delay!"

I picked up two pairs of blue jeans
That were lying on the floor,
And as I looked around my room,
I counted a dozen more.

My bedroom was so untidy,
Especially, my bedroom floor.
This was going to be hard work!
A real back-breaking chore!

But I knew that it was possible.
Somehow I'd get it done,
But how was I to clean this room?
Oh, this would be no fun!

If only I had a robot,
Or that cat with that tall hat,
A genie in a magic bottle,
Or something similar to that.

"A vacuum cleaner!" I shouted.
"Why, that might do the trick!
I'll vacuum everything!" I thought.
"But I'd better do it quick!"

So off I ran to the laundry room,
And I grabbed the vacuum cleaner.
Then I rushed back to my bedroom
And vacuumed a wrinkled wiener.

I vacuumed the dozen jeans
That were lying on the floor.
I vacuumed a number of dirty shirts,
And underwear . . . a whole lot more!

I vacuumed books and paper,
My train set and an old bookbag,
A very large number of peanuts shells,
And a dirty, old dingy rag.

Lorraine L. Hollowell

In no time at all my room was clean.
I was so proud of me . . .
Until I looked in a corner
And discovered a little green pea.

I'd get that pea; then I'd be done.
Yes, shortly, I could stop,
But when I vacuumed that little green pea,
The vacuum cleaner went POP!!!